JEREMY VOSS

BUSINESS INTELLIGENCE

The Ultimate Guide to Business Planning and Strategies by a Business Coach, Learn the Benefits of Hiring a Business Coach on How It Can Make Your Online Business a Success

Descrierea CIP a Bibliotecii Naționale a României
JEREMY VOSS
    BUSINESS INTELLIGENCE. The Ultimate Guide to Business Planning and Strategies by a Business Coach, Learn the Benefits of Hiring a Business Coach on How It Can Make Your Online Business a Success / Jeremy Voss. – Bucharest: Editura My Ebook, 2020
    ISBN

JEREMY VOSS

BUSINESS INTELLIGENCE

The Ultimate Guide to Business Planning and Strategies by a Business Coach, Learn the Benefits of Hiring a Business Coach on How It Can Make Your Online Business a Success

My Ebook Publishing House
Bucharest, 2020

CONTENTS

WILL YOUR BUSINESS BENEFIT
FROM A BUSINESS COACH

The economy goes up and down. Right now, it's not doing so well. In fact, most would say it has tanked. Managing your costs is important to your growth and survival, and when the economy is performing poorly, it is even more of a challenge. Experts say that 58% of companies have a shortfall in leaders and many companies are actually cutting their development budget as part of their cost cutting measures.

Before you make that cut, you might want to think long and hard about whether that's the right choice for your business. When you take development away from the executives, it can be detrimental. Leading is actually special skill. A key leader can find a business coach a very helpful tool to navigate through the storm and continue to grow and prosper.

Business Coaching and its Effects

Chances are more than 50% of your staff could benefit from business coaching and actually become motivated and energized again with a focus and a goal. Executive coaching involves working with the leaders of your company. These should be the people that are running in high gear. There are some key points where an executive coach can help leaders.

* Polish and fine tune their leadership skills
* Grow their leadership style
* Recalibrate what the success metrics look like
* Learn how to navigate through the times that are uncertain
* Lead teams with more motivation and power

The program that your business coach or executive coach puts together will be customized to the needs of your team and your leaders. Even leaders who are new to your team can find business coaching very beneficial.

The use of a business coach is still in its infancy. Businesses are often slow to make change, but those that are perceptive tend to think outside the box and use tools that can help them to make their business more successful. Business coaches and executive coaches can be beneficial to all sizes of business from the very small to the largest. They will benefit each business in their own unique way and that will depend on the current needs of the business are.

Whether it's a downturn in the economy or it's a struggle to get past a certain block; whether it's a desire to see your leaders think outside the box and grow or it's a desire to make sure that your staff are operating in their finest capacity; a business coach can help.

4 REASONS YOU SHOULD USE A BUSINESS COACH TO GET RESULTS

Business coaching is a modern day concept. Many businesses, especially those that think outside the box, are recognizing that having a business coach is a powerful tool that your business can take advantage of. Let's look at 4 reasons you should use a business coach.

#1 A Business Coach Can Show You how to Get Greater Returns With Less Work

You work way too many hours and you believe if you were to leave even for a short vacation, things might fall apart, but boy, you are ready to work less! You can call the coaching by many names – executive coaching, small business coaching, business coaching and there are others – bottom line is that any one of these can help your company to become far more efficient. That means you will work less hours and make more money. A business coach can help you turn your old business model into a new business model that's more powerful and profitable.

#2 Business Coaching Can Create More Profits

Are you ready to make more money? If you aren't making the profits you thought you would it's time to change that and turn things around. A business coach can help you do that. He or she can help you to jump start your business. Your business coach isn't there to make the decisions for you, but they are there to open you up and help you explore how you might reach the goals you have and make the profits you desire.

#3 Business Coaches Help You Develop Your Team

You are ready to build a team so that you can grow your business. That's great news. A business coach can help you recruit, train, and keep the right team members. When you build a team, it can motivate everyone and allow you to create a powerful team with the help of your business coach. You can create passion among your team members.

#4 Business Coaches Can Help You Find Your Passion

If you need to fall back in love with your business, a business coach is just the tool to help you do that. Overtime every business can become a bit mundane and a bit boring. Motivation is key to maintaining and growing a vision and passion. Whether you are building a simple marketing plan or a full business your business coach is an excellent sounding board and can be an invaluable tool and sounding board to help you get your passion back!

A business coach is a service you have to pay for and that can sometimes stop people from making the call. Using a business coach is a great investment in your future.

COACHING TO GET RESULTS

Coaching has become a leading resource that business leaders are taking advantage of to create highly successful businesses. The one misunderstanding is that to use a business coach your business needs to be larger, but that's not the case at all.

Coaching can help create clarity and direction in any size business. Working with a business coach can help to determine what it is you want to create, the reason it is important, and how you plan to reach that goal. It can help you to create an action plan and then achieve the goals you set.

If you had an empowering way that you could commit to and then achieve your business goals, would you not want to take advantage of it? Well you do, it's called business coaching.

Business Coaching Helps You to Become Clear on Your Goals

It is important that you are clear on what it is you want from your business along with how you plan to get it. Then you will need to determine what your commitment is. A business coach can help you to create clear goals and plans on achieving those goals.

Business Coaching Aids You to be Effective and Productive

When it comes to support, business coaching provides individual attention along with the challenge and objectiveness that are needed. A skilled business coach is very successful because he or she can:

* Inspire you to expand your solutions
* Keep you focused on your goals
* Make you accountable for your progress
* Support you through the change
* Remove any obstacles so that you can move forward
* Prioritize based on your values
* Challenges you to take the next step

Business Coaching Connects You to What's Important

Your business coach will help to build a foundation that's grounded so that you make decisions that are in alignment with your value system and what you value most. They will also help you to create a plan that will ensure your daily actions are in alignment with the values. This is the key to creating commitment breakthroughs.

A small business can benefit as much from a business coach as a larger business. Your business coach isn't there to make decisions for you, but rather to be a sounding board and to help guide you in the direction that is right for you and your business. Take advantage of outside help to grow your business.

HOW BUSINESS COACHING HELPS
LEADERSHIP TEAMS

Business coaching is an important tool that can offer a unique advantage if you want to coach your leadership teams, especially in a growing business. Business coaching can help to create an environment that is healthy for leadership growth that can play a key role as the business also grows.

It can help leaders to set strategic direction, develop marketing strategies and operating tactics in a low risk and non stressful manner that will improve the numbers and create a business that can run without being dependent on the owner or CEO.

The training manual used by the business coach should walk through the needs of the company. The business coach should also ensure that the members of the leadership team have their needs explored, their skills analyzed and their goals discussed. In that way, it's easier to make sure your leadership team members are strategically placed to maximize the benefits to the company and create the best environment for the leaders.

You should not confuse coaching with training, as they are different, especially when it comes to the delivery system. A coach will work with management to tailor a training program in the skill areas where there is a need for impact. The coach will also help managers to make behavioral changes that are seen as necessary for growth. The significance is that the coach and the manager(s) must be clear on the competencies that will have an effect on the bottom line. It ism essential that the competencies are measured before and after coaching so that there can be an evaluation of the effectiveness.

At the beginning the relationship is determined – is the coach considered a trusted friend or an advisor? Does the coach listen and provide feedback or does the coach help the manager obtain 360-degree feedback and then develop an action plan to increase performance? The role and the relationship need to be established by both parties before the coaching project begins.

The coach will push the window with each manager to help them grow professionally and to promote the company's success and the success of the leadership team. A good way to do this is to create a situation so that each leadership team member will ask for help from the coach, rather than the coach forcing their help on the manager.

Business coaching doesn't look just one way. It is designed to be created to work specific to the needs of the client and in doing so the delivery can be tailor made.

HOW BUSINESS COACHING WORKS

We hear a lot about business coaching these days, but you may not actually understand how it works and what it's really all about. In fact, you may have considered business coaching, but then changed your mind because you weren't really sure your company needed it.

Business coaching will apply the essential coaching principles to every part of a business or organization. It will follow meticulous and detailed methodology to ensure both facilitative coaching processes and management consulting tools are employed and put into place in the manner they should be.

It is acknowledged just how important the role of employee productivity is to any business or organization. Therefore, it is also interesting and important to know about the productivity components and their role in the business success.

Employees at every level of the organization must have the proper skill and the skills they have must be properly used.

Employees need to be motivated in order for optimal productivity to occur and for the corporations or organizations' vision to be fulfilled.

The matching of skill and experience of employees to positions within the company or organization is generally managed through the HR department that is responsible for creating the HR processes including recruitment and training. Management teams usually manage the planning and use of staff to get the highest production. However, few companies actually manage employee motivation very well. It is rarely recognized or understood. Recent motivational studies that have been done by Harvard research confirm this.

Motivating your employees by throwing incentives at them, can work for a short time; however, if you want sustainable motivation there must be an alignment between the employee's personal goals and aspirations and the company's needs. This alignment is what the business coaching process can do for a business or organization and it is also where the success lies.

The Business Coaching Process

There is really no such thing as a generic business coaching process. Solutions should be catered to each businesses needs. The process will look much different for a company that is restructuring one department than a company that is undertaking a cultural shift throughout the organization.

Business coaching is a powerful tool that can transform a business form just surviving to highly successful. It can help to change the way processes flow within an organization or create an entirely new workplace environment. Business coaching is limited only by your needs and your budget. There are few companies that can't benefit from an outsiders viewpoint and skills.

Business coaching can be a valuable investment.

HIGHLY EFFECTIVE BUSINESS COACHING

Business coaching – what is it? Executives and managers of companies who are interested in development and career growth increasingly turn to a business coach to have a customized development process. Consider this – how often would you have found it helpful to have a chance to talk about some key ideas with a person that is impartial and objective in preparation for a major change or perhaps a very important meeting.

The concept of business coaching has actually come from the sports arena where top athletes employ coaches to help improve and enhance their performance. Business people are slowly realizing that the same benefits can be enjoyed in the business arena using business coaches.

Coaching works best in those environments where there is a desire to be practical, progressive and proactive but at the same time there is value in the opportunity to challenge and

22

stimulate. The executive(s) or manager(s) is thought to be the expert in his/her field and in this way the business coach will facilitated the executive or manager to find the right way forward. Coaching is always forward thinking with a well-structured approach that remains flexible and presumes purpose and commitment.

Effective, Efficient, Productive

When it comes to professional support, business coaching is the exception as it combines individual attention, challenge and objectiveness. The coach's skills make it extremely successful because:

- It inspires you to develop your own solutions
- It keeps you focusing on a specific goal or goals It makes you accountable for your progress
- It supports you through change
- It removes any blockages so that you can move forward It prioritizes based on values
- It challenges you to take the next step in moving forward

Research published in Olivero et al. 1997 showed that training can increase productivity by as much as 22 percent, but when training is combined with coaching, it can increase productivity by a whopping 88 percent.

What Does Business Coaching Involve?

Coaching is not training – the delivery system is much different. A business coach will work with the executive or manager to develop a training program that is tailored to the skill areas where there is a need for impact. The coach will help the executive/manager to make the necessary behavioral changes to create growth. The coach does not provide the answer, but rather the coach brings along a process or system to help the client determine the answers.

HOW BUSINESS COACHING CAN CREATE CONTINUALLY MOTIVATED EMPLOYEES

Those companies that are highly effective take great pains to make sure that they have established a clear vision for their company along with a clear and concise strategy of how they want to implement that vision. They carefully recruit and retain those employees who are the best to help them carry out their strategy. After all, it is common sense that if you want your company to have a high degree of success you need to have high and continuous employee production, because you can't do it alone. This means you also have continually motivate employees.

By definition, employee motivation is a key component of the employee productivity equation. It is in this area where you will find that business coaching can have the biggest impact. You can temporarily boost your employees' motivation using incentives, especially financial incentives, but these are not sustainable employee motivation methods and they will stop working.

Business coaching can help you to create sustainable employee motivation.

A company establishes its vision, mission and execution strategy. An employee also needs to establish their own vision. It will just be minus all the corporate 'talk,' and it will be their terms, what they want out of their career at the company.

A business coach will support employees using a mix of individual sessions and group sessions. They will help employees to articulate what it is they want, their goals, and then help them to determine how they might reach those goals in relation to the company they work for.

Employees usually find these types of sessions far more useful than when companies use 'Personal Development Plan' templates. Actually, when the results are structured right, they can actually take the templates and transfer them to work effectively for personal development.

Facilitative coaching sessions will take a bottom up data approach that details the skills of each employee and what their motivators are to reconcile with the objectives of the business. The focus is to align corporate objectives to the needs of the employees.

Of course, not all employees will get what it is they want. It will be up to your management team to negotiate a solution that is a win-win for everyone involved. Management will also have to effectively create the basis for the sustainable employee motivation to get the most out of the process.

A LOOK AT THE DIFFERENT
COACHING STYLES

Many people are unaware that there are a number of different coaching styles that can be used by a coach. Let's have a look at some of these different coaching styles.

* **Traditional Coaching Model** - The coach identifies with how the client is feeling. The coach acts as a guide and confidant.

* **Advanced Coaching Model** - Useful when there is a need to make a considerable break from the past, and where the person wants to try new things or a new way of doing something.

* **Block Removal Coaching** - This coaching model works when a person is resistant to growth, which causes a block, that usually the result of a hidden fear or limiting beliefs.

* **Innovation Coaching Model** - This coaching model focuses on experimentation, creativity and innovation.

* **3-D Coaching Model -** This coaching model works on who a person is and what they want, then how to get it.

* **Personal Foundation Model** - The coach will work on standards and boundaries. The higher a person wants to go, the deeper the foundation has to be.

* **Bigger Thinking Model** - The coach will challenge the person's assumptions and work to break one out of their comfort zone and expand their thinking!

* **Solution Coaching** - The coach will identify symptoms, find out the source of those symptoms, and then work with a person to find a solution.

* **Shift Coaching Model** - When a person isn't able to determine how to achieve their goals, a shift in thinking can help. The coach can help a person to step back, shift, and then move forward.

* **Deep Coaching** - There can be a shift in basic beliefs over time until these beliefs simply are not true any longer. The coach can help a person dig deep to discover the 'out of date truth' which a person can then align with the reality of today.

* **Performance Coaching Model** - For the client that is competitive, the coach can help by developing a persuasive goal, creating milestones to help you focus on your goals, and building momentum through reporting daily.
* **Acceptance Coaching Model** - Rather than a person trying to overcome a weakness, the coach can help to accept it and use it to their advantage.
* **Intermediate Model** - A good model when a person wants the coach to work in partnership on developing goals and then on achieving them.

As you can see, there are many different ways that business coaching can be approached. It can pay to match the coach's style with your needs to get the best results. Talk to the coach you are considering hiring and see what style they use. Don't be afraid to ask questions so you make the right choice.

COACHING MODELS FOR THE WORKPLACE

The earliest coaching models date back the 1950s and through the 1980s, they were still static models. It wasn't until the 1990s, when sports coaching models began to grow in popularity. A coaching model needs to be flexible and adaptable so that it can be tailored to the specific needs of the client. Today's coaching model should:

* Presents a complete, detailed description of the process that's involved
* It should build towards an outcome that's predicted
* It should establish the nature of the components
* It uses valid methodology to produce change that is sustainable and measurable

The traditional coaching model was built around change models that were outdated like the grow model, action planning, goal setting, etc. fall very short of creating lasting behavior

31

competencies that are measurable. Using a 'one size fits all' approach is simplistic and ineffective because it ignores the person's behavioral pattern that controls how the skill that's going to be improved is executed.

With traditional coaching very shortly after those who participated revert back to their old behaviors after the event. It seems it's a pretty expensive venture for a quick buzz that fades fast. The challenge for development professionals is to improve the organization's effectiveness through behavioral change that involves a learning model that strengthens the individuals and sustains the behavioral skills.

The 21st century professional coaching is a combined approach that the behavioral sciences founded. Today's coaching model includes personal beliefs, development, attitudes, values, motivation, social learning and emotions along with organizational and personal dynamics.

Many mechanisms of the behavioral based coaching model come from the behavioral approach to learning and changing. Some of the coaching model aspects are:

* Targeting and then focusing on an explicit behavior
* Analyzing a behavior in relation to its precursor and the consequences

* Applying a reliable and valid method of data collection, data analysis and assessment
* Building of a developmental plan
* Employing behavioral change techniques that are validated
* Measuring, managing and maintaining behavioral change

Coaching models for the workplace need to be effective long term. They shouldn't provide the answers, but rather the circumstances for the participant(s) to come up with their own solutions that will work. The coach is a bit like a sounding board opening up a dialogue that will help the participants to grow and prosper and that can help a business to grow and prosper as well.

HOW ONE ON ONE BUSINESS
COACHING CAN HELP

Business coaches can be a powerful tool for any business environment. They can help business managers in innovative companies to understand and take the next step in solving a specific technology or business development. A business coach can help your company reach the next stage in product development.

When business coaching is done on a one on one basis it can be offered in many forms such as weekly or monthly and each session can last from a couple of hours to a full day. Monthly programs tend to work well with small to mid size businesses where there is only one owner or one partner. The company's commitment to business coaching should be long term. On average 9 to 12 months is the commitment period. Most business coaches can create custom packages for you.

ROI for the Business Owner

Using the unique approach of having a business coach work with your management team or other employees, can be highly beneficial to your ROI. The increase in profitability using a business coach is well documented. Business coaching can result in a larger market share, improved talent retention, lower operating costs, improved marketing, faster methods to get the product to market, greater customer satisfaction and overall streamlining. The use of personal that's from outside the organization can help you to see things differently and help you to grow and prosper.

You Have the Choice

The business coaches one of the most powerful word is 'choice.' A person can choose to make change, to grow, to learn, to evolve. In fact, no matter what your choice is, change is going to occur. The change will bring about a new environment and it can reunite your passion and change your perception, which becomes your reality. Innovative leadership is a powerful tool for any business.

Business coaching does a great job of increasing self awareness, and helping a business owner see how they are being perceived and then redefine that perception. A business coach can help you to identify the core strengths and core behaviors of the management and leadership team to ensure all involved clearly understand how to select and optimize the most powerful asset any business has – that is the human potential. The reality is the success or failure of any business comes down to the humans that are involved and the decisions that are made.

Coaching allows you to look at old habits and then choose new ones that are more powerful strategies.

THE ONE ON ONE COACHING MODEL

The one on one coaching model is an excellent choice if you want to invest in the talent for the future. It can play a positive role in the long-term strategy and yet often it is a strategy that's overlooked. The coaching relationship is going to enhance the skills that are needed during difficult and changing times. When your company invests in this type of development of company talent, they are looking at a long-term strategy for their company and one that can be created using the one on one coaching model. It looks similar to this.

* The coach will meet with the manager(s) and Human Resource Dept. to talk about the goals of the candidate and they will come to an agreement on the targets.
* The coach will meet with the candidate to collect personal history, career data and then to reach an agreement on the goals and expectations.

* The assessment process will begin by using a variety of instruments along with the 360 feedback from employees that work in close proximity with the candidate.
* Feedback is collected and then it is analyzed to decide on assets and liabilities, which are then presented to the candidate.
* The candidate will create a developmental plan that's specific to behavior and determine the desired outcome that will also include input from the manager and/or Human Resources personal.
* The plan is implemented so that it also has time frames and suitable tools.
* The coach works with the candidate to incorporate the new behaviors with the regular one-on- one sessions.
* The coach will reassess the close-working employees, and then evaluate and report the incremental shifts. Engagement will extend when there is revised objectives.

Choosing a Coach

Choosing the right coach is important. It means you need to find out who best fits the candidate. Personalities vary, but still professionals should be able to blend with a mix of personalities. A professional coach should have these qualifications:

* Experience in the industry.
* Exposure to working with senior staff and the types of issues they face.
* Exposure to and/or certification in numerous assessment tools.
* Being able to provide feedback.
* Five or more years of corporate coaching are preferred.
* Expertise and significant exposure in organizational changes.

You've heard it before – when the going gets tough the tough get going, or they should take advantage of one on one coaching to help create opportunities and make goals. A coach is able to reinforce the needed skills for both current personal and new personnel so that they can move forward.

THE ROLE OF THE BUSINESS COACH
PUT INTO PLAY

The concept of business coaching actually got its start on the sports field. In sports, top athletes have coaches to help improve their performance and enhance their abilities. That concept has been transposed to the players in the business arena who have realized that the same methodology can apply in the business environment. Executives and managers can improve their performance and enhance their skills by having a business coach.

Initially a meeting needs to be established with the business coach who will assist in identifying the requirements so that a specific program can be created to meet those requirements.

Coaching can also be extended out to employee groups or kept at the individual level. The business coach isn't there to bring the answers. Their role is to bring a process or a system that will help the client to discover their own answers.

Accepted as a Coach

An effective coach will define the relationship right at the beginning. The role could be that of a trusted advisor or friend, it could as a sounding board and to provide feedback, it could be as a performer to help create a plan. This needs to be established early and this role must accepted by both parties if it's going to work.

The coach will push the envelope with each manager he/she works with so that they can grow professionally and play a major role in both the company's success and their individual success.

The Coach Isn't the One in Control

It is important to remember that the coach is a resource and he/she is not in control of the relationship, the decisions or the actions of the person being coached. Sometimes the coach does form a partnership with the coached manager that helps develop good decisions and choices for the company and the manager's personal growth. However, ultimately the manager will make the final decisions, not the coach. Your effectiveness as a communicator and your knowledge along with the relationship you have developed will ultimately play a role in whether a manager chooses to incorporate any recommendations you might have.

The role of the coach should be clear. As important as the coach can be to a company and the management and staff, they are the outsider looking in and it is very important that clear and concise guidelines are established from the very beginning to make sure that no lines are crossed.

HOW YOUR BUSINESS COACH CAN HELP YOU GROW YOUR BUSINESS

Your business is doing okay, but you'd like to see it grow and prosper. That doesn't seem to be happening. If you are wondering what you should do, it's a place many business owners find themselves. A good place to start is with a business coach, who can help you to grow your business.

A Business Coach Helps You to Navigate Market and Economic Changes

You are very aware that you need to grow your business, but for that to happen and for you to grow you will have to learn more. It's hard keeping up with changes in the industry, never mind the changes that occurring on a global business scale. Trying to figure out how to improve your role in the mix can be a bit daunting. Business education is now in a new realm with business coaching and business mentoring replacing the more traditional form of consulting, seminars and books. So if you want to get it right it's time to turn to your business coach.

Business Coaches Can Establish Accountability

Your business coach is going to hold you accountable, to demand you see results and to demand you see a profit. Your business coach is someone who can push you, challenge you, encourage you to think outside the box, and congratulate you when you succeed. It can be a lonely job being the owner and you often don't have the sounding board that you desire or need. A trained business coach can help you to solve the problems that arise and to turn these situations into opportunities.

Business Coaches Can Offer You a Second Opinion From Another Expert

You need a business coach to demand results and hold you accountable. You need a business coach who can see through the maze and who isn't blinded by the industry or that fact that there is too much competition. You want a business coach who can keep his or her eye on the prize. That's a powerful combination for you.

Like your life, running your business can be challenging and there can certainly be ups and down. Sometimes it's the simplest of things that hang you up and you can't work your way through it. A business coach cannot only offer you a second opinion, they can be a great sounding board to help you get over your stumbling block.

Why not join the thousands of small businesses that are turning to business coaches for help growing their business.

Training Methods and Techniques Used By Business Coaches

In order for a business to transform into a great business, it will have to recognize the strengths of the people that work for the company. Bottom line – your company is only as good as the people you have working for you. If you want to unleash the full power of your company, it will have to begin with the individual.

When the individuals, employees are shown how to self manage and to upgrade their professional skill set as well as their personal skill set; and when they learn how to feel alert, balanced, powerful and in control; it is then that they will have the largest contribution to your company. When your company is able to move its people into an optimum zone, with sustainable top performance, the company will also have top performance.

There are many different training techniques and methods that can be used. The focus is on developing further the employee's thinking skill set and to give them the edge. Here are just a few tips and tricks to consider incorporating into the training.

MAKE SURE THAT THE TRAINING
TECHNIQUES AND METHODS

* Will improve the employee's overall well-being. This includes immediate performance and long-term.
* Are filled with fast paced learning that's fun and relevant to 'real life' experiences and that everyone can immediately.
* Will provide positive changes in the thinking skills of employees that affect their professional skills.
* Are loyal to the employers and build exceptional goodwill throughout the organization.
* Integrates well with other development and training initiatives.
* This will cost significantly less than other comparable development and training solutions.

Benefits to the Workplace

* An increase in productivity
* Challenges you to take the next step
* Learning to maximize the workload in the workplace
* Minimize the stress in the workplace
* Help to find focus and build self confidence
* Prioritize based on your values
* Improved career direction
* Employees experience more fulfillment
* Employee enlightenment
* Inspire you to expand your solutions
* Remove any obstacles so that you can move forward
* Keep you focused on your goals
* Make you accountable for your progress
* Support you through the change

There are numerous training methods and techniques used by business coaches in the workplace. No one method is right or wrong, but it is helpful when the business coach are able to cater their training methods to the environment.

UNDERSTANDING THE ROLE
OF THE BUSINESS COACH

The business coach is an important asset that savvy businesses and organizations are taking advantage of their services. Still, many don't fully understand the role of the business coach in today's modern business, so let's have a look.

#1 A Business Coach Supports the Employee

It's usually executives or managers that seek guidance or input from a coach when they are not sure how to handle a certain situation. Sometimes help is sought before a tentative or difficult situation is dealt with. Managers will often seek assistance with their own growth as a manager, which can leave coaches with a very difficult and delicate situation.

A coach has the ability to improve the executive's abilities and self esteem, especially if there is confirmation that his or her answer is right. If a coach doesn't know what the right answer or is speculating the correct course of action is the truth. It's far better to say you do not know than to give bad advice.

#2 A Business Coach Helps Manager to Develop Their Solutions

People usually know how to act or what they should do. Many time's the job of the coach is to draw out the answer from the person, because if you give him/her the answer then they are less likely to own the solution. A coach can offer options and make resource recommendations, even give opinions. A coach can answer questions, but in the end the manager must have the answer.

#3 A Coach Must Have Communication Skills That Are Sharpened

Listening is a key skill all coaches need to have in order to be able to understand the actual needs of the manager who is asking for their assistance. It is a coach weakness when he or she assumes the current situation or question is like one previously encountered. The coach needs to be fully engaged and aware to take in the information that is being provided.

Open ended questions are necessary to draw out the manager. Listening includes watching body language, facial expression, tone of voice, and movements.

#4 A Coach is a Teacher or Educator

As an external coach you teach managers and leaders as you work with them. The goal is to make them self sufficient. The role of the coach is to provide them with the tools they need to be successful in their business arena.

WHAT IS BUSINESS COACHING
AND HOW CAN IT BENEFIT YOUR BUSINESS

Business coaching – you may have heard a lot of buzz around it, but might still not be sure exactly what it is. A business coach is like a mentor that can help you and your business. Your focus and your goal is to grow your business, increase your profits and be highly successful.

You might have lots of ideas on how to take your business to the next level, but wouldn't it be helpful if you had someone you could bounce those ideas of that was objective and impartial? Wouldn't it be beneficial to have someone to talk to about key ideas to make major changes to your business? That's where a business coach can help. They aren't there to give you the answers. They are there to help you work through your ideas and answers to find clarity and move forward.

Business coaching is most effective when those involved want to be practical and progressive while at the same time being proactive rather than reactive. A business coach will be most effective those who like to be stimulated and challenged. As a business owner, this likely describes you and so you can see why the use of a business coach could be highly beneficial to you and your company. Business coaching is structured forward thinking that is also flexible with commitment and purpose.

Business coaching is so successful because it:
* Will motivate you to create solutions
* Will help you to focus on your specific goals
* Will make you accountable for the progress you do or do not make
* Will support you through the transition
* Will remove any stumbling blocks so you can move forward
* Will help you to prioritize
* Will challenge you to move forward

Do not confuse training with coaching. The way it is delivered is significantly different. A business coach will work with you to create a training program for your company. That training program will be tailored to meet the needs of your business. The skills that are needed to grow your business will be addressed. Your business coach will make changes to help take your business to the next step. The coach doesn't have the answers, you do and he or she will help you to bring those ideas to life. Now that you know exactly what a business coach is, the time might be now to use their services.

USING REFLECTIVE LANGUAGE IN BUSINESS COACHING

Business coaching is a powerful tool, and it becomes even more useful when reflective language is used, which is the reflecting back of what the coach says in his or her own words. This leads to a win-win situation, ideal for success.

With reflective language, the coach isn't using mental activity to interpret and there is no need for the coach to become detached from their experience because they are worried about the meaning of the coach's words. The best coaches use reflective language and while the coaches might not notice when reflective language is used, those observing most certainly do.

The reflective language is intended to help the employees stay connected to their discovery process. The words expressed are then reflected back in as perfect a form as possible so that there is no need to translate them.

Words are let out and then reflected right back, without any resistance. The coach never once questions the words because the words are theirs. The process of reflective questioning is so perfect that the employee doesn't even notice the sentence construction and they are able to stay focused on their own thinking and discovery evolution.

Sub Modalities

Sub modalities a just experience variants. In coaching, there is the possibility of extending the employee's experiences in the world by inviting the audience to focus on their experiences and then play them. This isn't a new concept dating back to the 1960s, but it still remains important today. When you explore the sub modalities of experiences it can lead to a change in visual and auditory representation.

When you watch a person's language, you will get clues on how they store information. Inviting an employee to experiment with sub modalities of their experience can help them to find ways that are more constructive to manage situations in the future and it can provide a routine support system for those tough scenarios.

Sub modalities can be a bit hard to understand, but there is a great deal of information available online that will help you to better understand. You will even be able to find some working examples.

Reflective language is a powerful tool that business coaches can use when working with employees. It's a tool that is often overlooked and yet has so much value. Business coaching is a powerful tool that most companies can really benefit from.

WHAT IS BUSINESS COACHING
AND WHAT CAN IT DO FOR YOU

Coaching is a process that enables executives, managers and staff to achieve their full potential. Coaching and mentoring are similar in nature. Let's look at some of the things your business coach will do for you, your staff and your business.

* Will teach clients to creatively apply techniques and tools. This includes things like facilitating, doing one-on-one training, counseling and networking.

* Encourages clients to a commitment to action and the development of growth and change that's lasting.

* Encouraging clients to constantly advance competencies and to expand developmental association whenever necessary to attain their goals.

* Ensure that clients build their personal competencies and that they don't build unhealthy dependencies on the coaching relationship.

* Evaluate the outcome of the process, with the use of objective measures when possible to make sure the relationship thrives and the client is achieving their goals both personal and work related.

* Facilitate the exploration of the clients needs, desires, motivations, skills and the thought process to assist the client in making real and lasting changes.

* Preserve positive unconditional regard for the client, which means that the coach is always non judgmental and supportive of the client, their aspirations and views.

* Management of the relationship to make sure the client get a suitable level of service and that the program isn't too long or too short.

* Observe the client, listen and ask questions to understand the situation of the client.

* Use questioning techniques to make possible the client's own thought processes to identify solutions and actions rather than using a direct approach.

* Proven coaching training practices can bolster trust, strengthen relationships and commitment, and enjoy the benefits of open communication.

* Give meaningful feedback to clients on the best way to communicate requests and suggestions to others?

* Provide skill to build trust and acceptance.

* Teach clients how to use questions to achieve the best performance.

* Examine the behaviors that will lead to unreliable behavior and the inability to achieve the client's goals.

Business coaching is a valuable tool where a trained professional comes into a business no matter what the business size to work with executives, managers, and staff so that they can create their goals and achieve those goals, so that they can grow and expand their skills and improve their role in the workplace achieving their goals.

WHY USING A BUSINESS COACH CAN GET YOU THE RESULTS YOU WANT

The modern day business looks much different than it did a few decades ago and business coaching is a relatively new concept too. It's been proven to be highly valuable and effective, which is why so many businesses today find business coaches a powerful tool that can help grow their business. Businesses that are more forward thinking are quick to recognize the benefits of using a business coach.

Businesses want to grow their profits. After all, that's what business is about right. If you are ready to see your bottom line grow and you aren't satisfied with your current bottom line, you might consider using a business coach who can aid in giving your business a boost. Your business coach isn't there to make decisions for you. Instead the role of the business coach is to help you open up and to aid you in exploring how you can reach your goals and make the profit you desire.

Using a business coach can help you to discover how you can work less and make more. There's this mistaken identity with the harder you work the better. But actually most people work too many hours, don't take enough vacations and don't get the rest they need. Things can start to fall apart if you aren't taking care of yourself. A business coach can help you discover how you can work less and make more, turning over a new leaf from your old business model to a new business model that's more profitable.

A business coach can help you to develop your team and grow your business, helping you to train and recruit the right members for your team. Building a strong team is a good way to motivate everyone in the team and it allows for the creation of a very powerful team that's passionate.

It's pretty common for a person to lose their passion over time. The same applies to you and your business. Whether it's you as the business own that's lost your passion or your staff that boredom and mundane behavior can jeopardize the success and growth of any business.

Motivation is behind every passion and every vision. Your business coach can help motivate you and/or staff again by becoming the sounding board for new ideas. Bring the passion into your business and watch it grow.

WHY YOU WANT TO HIRE THE SERVICES OF A BUSINESS COACH

You are ready to take your business to the next level. Sure, it's healthy, but you also realize that without growth that it will stagnate and could also become nonviable. Yet, so far you just can't seem to make it happen. You just haven't been able to take it to the next level. The time is now – hire a business coach to help you expand and grow your business.

We are all familiar with sports coaches. They help athletes to perform their best. Well a business coach is the equivalent in the business world. A business coach can help you navigate through the ups and downs of a changing economy and a changing market. May times the missing component to a growing business is knowledge. As you learn more about your industry, the global market and your role in the mix you will be able to make sound decisions on your growth.

A business coach can help you to do that through business education, which is accomplished through business coaching and replacing a more conventional method of learning that involves seminars, books and consulting. If you want to get the advantage over the competition turn to a business coach.

Your business coach isn't going to create solutions for you. They are going to be a sounding board for you and they are going to hold you accountable for results. Expect your business coach to push you, encourage you and challenge you to open up your thinking to look outside the box and most importantly to succeed. As an owner, you already know it's lonely at the top and many times you don't have anyone to bounce ideas off or talk through those ideas. A business coach can be that person. They can also help you problem solve and turn problems into opportunities.

Having a business coach working with you gives you a chance for a second option from another highly respected professional. Your business coach should help you navigate the maze and when you hire a business coach, they can help you to keep your focus on the reward at the end of the tunnel – the increased profits.

You're a business owner and that can be challenging. Every business has it's good times and low times. Sometimes the problem is an easy fix other times it requires more in-depth thinking and it can be what holds your business back. Having a business coach can be just what you need to remove the obstacle and see clearly what needs to occur for you to move forward, grow your business and increase your profits.

Printed by Libri Plureos GmbH in Hamburg, Germany